A⁺
Smart Apple Media

Smart Apple Media is published by Black Rabbit Books
P.O. Box 3263, Mankato, Minnesota 56002

Printed in the United States

Published by arrangement with the Watts Publishing Group Ltd, London.

Library of Congress Cataloging-in-Publication Data

Butterfield, Moira, 1961–
    Lady of the manor / Moira Butterfield.
    p. cm. — (Smart apple media. Medieval lives)
    Summary: "Traces the life of a typical medieval lady of the manor (the wife of a knight and second in command on his estate) from birth to death, including childhood, marriage, the duties of a wife, raising children, and hobbies. Includes primary source quotes"—Provided by publisher.
    Includes index.
    ISBN 978-1-59920-169-6
    1. Women—Europe—History—Middle Ages, 500-1500. 2. Social history—Medieval, 500-1500. I. Title.
HQ1143.B87 2009
305.4086'210940902—dc22

2008000443

Artwork: Gillian Clements
Editor: Sarah Ridley
Editor in chief: John C. Miles
Designer: Simon Borrough
Art director: Jonathan Hair
Picture research: Diana Morris

Picture credits:
Abbaye de L'Epau Loire/Gianni Dagli Orti/The Art Archive: 41. Arquivo Nacional da Torre do Tombo Lisbon/Alfredo Dagli Orti/The Art Archive: 24. The Art Archive: 4,16. Biblioteca d'Ajuda Libon/Gianni Dagli Orti/The Art Archive: 32. Biblioteca Nazionale Marciana Venice/The Art Archive: 18. Bibliothèque Saint-Genieve Paris/ Bridgeman Art Library : 13. Bodleian Library Oxford/The Art Archive: 30, 36. The British Library London/The Art Archive: 12, 17, 20, 31, 38. The British Library London/HIP/Topfoto:front cover, 10, 25, 27, 33, 34, 35, 37. Centre Historiques des Archives Nationales Paris/Giraudon Lauros/Bridgeman Art Library: 40. Jim Cole/Alamy: 14. Eric Lessing/AKG Images: 9. Eric Lessing/Musée Condé Chantilly/AKG Images: 23. Musée Condé Chantilly/AKG Images: 29. Musée Condé Chantilly/Bridgeman Art Library: 26. Museo de Arte Antiga Lisbon/Alfredo Dagli Orti/The Art Archive: 28. Museum of London/Bridgeman Art Library: 19.

9 8 7 6 5 4 3 2 1

CONTENTS

A Medieval Lady　　8

Beginnings　　10

Invitation to a Wedding　　12

At Home　　14

Being a Wife　　16

Noble Children　　18

A Year in the Life　　20

Clothes and Hairstyles　　22

Sports and Hobbies　　24

Books　　26

Time to Eat　　28

Treating Illness　　30

Women Who Work　　32

The Noblest Ladies　　34

The Lady and the Nuns　　36

The World Outside　　38

Widowhood　　40

Glossary　　42

Time Line/Useful Web Sites　　43

Index　　44

A MEDIEVAL LADY

The medieval period of European history is from approximately 1000 to 1500. This was the era of knights and their ladies. Many knights left their ladies in charge while they fought in a series of wars between France and England, called the Hundred Years' War, or went on crusades to fight the Muslim Arab armies for control of Jerusalem. This book follows the life of a lady of the manor. Although she never existed, her tale is based on the facts we know about medieval women's lives.

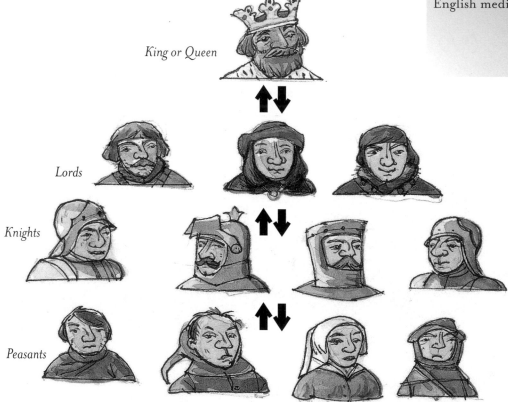

King or Queen

Lords

Knights

Peasants

Feudal Society

Medieval society was made up of different classes—groups of people at different social levels. The king was the most powerful, and he owned all the land. Next in rank were the lords, important nobles who were given land by the king in return for service. This meant fighting for him a certain number of days a year. When called to fight, they had to bring a number of fighting men, including their knights. The knights were lesser-ranked nobles who owed fighting service to a lord. They were "dubbed," which means they were given the rank of knight in an official ceremony. A lord could grant a knight an estate, made up of properties and land, in return for fighting a certain number of days a year. The knight then rented his land out to tenants, often peasants, in return for regular payments of money, crops, or work service.

Introducing Ladies

A knight's title was "Sir." The wife of a knight could use the title of "Lady." Generally, she would be the daughter of another knight, so she was from a noble family. She would be the top-ranking female on her husband's estate—the lady of the manor. Her husband was considered to be more important. He owned everything on his estate. By law, everything she owned belonged to him. But she ranked second on the estate and was his deputy. When he went away to fight, she managed the daily life of the estate, also called the manor.

Born a Lady

Our imaginary lady of the manor is English and was born in 1291 when Edward I was king. At 13, she marries a knight and leaves her family's manor to live on his manor. It is not too far from her old home. Her husband's family are friends of her father, and his land is in a neighboring area. The bride has been taught from childhood what behavior is expected of a lady. Her parents selected her husband for her. She knew from the age of seven whom she would marry when she was old enough. She was born to be a lady of the manor and has no choice.

This fine, lifelike thirteenth-century statue of a noble lady—Uta of Ballenstedt—is in the cathedral in Naumburg, Germany. She and her husband, the Margrave, gave money to help build the cathedral.

9

BEGINNINGS

The baby girl is born in her parents' manor house. Some women from the nearby village help during the birth. The baby's mother has already had four children. Two have survived; the other two died young. The baby is born upstairs in the solar, the lord of the manor's private family room. Everyone prays she will be strong. On average, two or three out of every ten medieval children die before the age of five. Another two or three die before reaching adulthood.

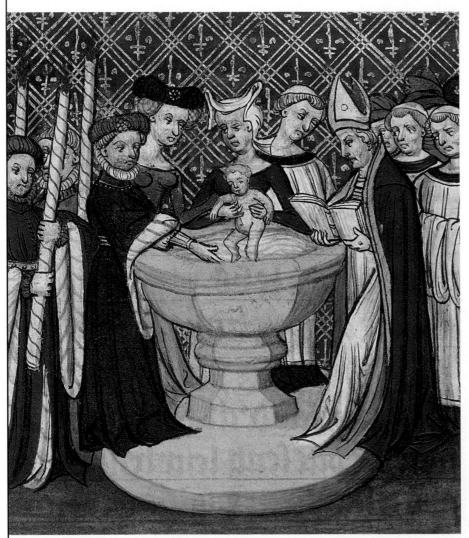

A medieval noble baby is baptized at the font by a bishop.

An Urgent Blessing

The baby is baptized as soon as she is born. This means she is blessed by a churchman and made a member of the Catholic Church, the only recognized religion. There is no time to lose. The church teaches that if she dies unbaptized, there will be no place for her in heaven. Unbaptized babies cannot be buried in holy ground. Once she is born and baptized, the baby's little limbs are gently massaged with a honey and salt mixture. This helps to get rid of any skin infections. Then she is swaddled (wrapped tightly) in bandages to keep her from wriggling around and hurting herself. It is believed that this will help her limbs grow straight.

Medieval Childhood

The baby grows into a little girl who spends her days playing around the manor house and in the kitchen gardens. As she grows older, her mother and her mother's female attendants teach her what well-born ladies ought to know—

Medieval Facts

The Catholic Church taught that unbaptized children went to "limbo" when they died, which is a miserable place between heaven and hell. In an emergency, a midwife was allowed to baptize a baby if no churchman was available. Midwives can still do this today.

reading, writing, manners, embroidery, singing, and playing musical instruments.

When her brothers turn seven, they are sent away to live in the house of another knight. They become pages and learn how to be a knight. Neighboring knights send a couple of their boys to be pages in her home. Her mother teaches them manners and her father begins to teach them what is expected of a knight.

Males Come First

The little girl will not inherit her father's lands when he dies because her brothers come before her by law. But she will be given some land, called a "dower," which she will inherit from her mother. One day, she will pass this on to her daughter. She does inherit her father's coat-of-arms and can combine it with her husband's when she marries. This becomes her personal coat-of-arms that she can use on her clothing and, perhaps, have carved onto a wall where she lives.

If she was an only child, she would inherit everything from her father. But this could be a disaster for the family if she was an only child and her father died before she married. The king could take payment from her guardian. The guardian could take the profits from her estate or sell off parts of her estate until the day she married.

The future lady of the manor plays in the garden with her nurse.

Custody

An unfortunate widow is reminded that custody of her young children and her dead husband's lands has been given to a guardian by the king. To get them back, she would have to offer payment.

❖ *To Mabel, late the wife of Richard De Torpel. She must well remember that the King gave the custody of the land and heirs of the said Richard De Torpel to the Bishop of Chichester.* ❖

INVITATION TO A WEDDING

When she was 7, the young girl was betrothed to a young nobleman of 13. Neither of them had a say in the matter; it was arranged between the two families. Now she is 13 and it is time for the betrothed couple to marry. Before the twelfth century, they could have been married anywhere—under a tree or in a house—without the Catholic Church being involved. But now, in 1304, the marriage ceremony will take place in the church.

Betrothal

It is six years since the betrothal ceremony took place before witnesses. If either family had chose to break the betrothal without agreement, they could have ended up in court. The young nobleman is 20. He has become a knight and inherited his father's estate. The young lady will bring her dowry into the marriage. The financial agreement between the families represents her share of her father's inheritance. Her dowry consists of some goods, money, and her dower land.

Wedding Day

Before the wedding, the banns are read three times in the local church. If anyone has evidence that the planned marriage is illegal, they declare it at this time. The bride and groom meet at the church door for the service. The groom announces what has been agreed on as the bride's dowry. He gives her some gold or silver and a ring, which is laid on a book. They make vows to each other and then go inside the church. They say prayers and kneel under a holy

The noble couple meet at the door of the church to exchange vows.

cloth, or pall, to have their marriage blessed. After the wedding, there is a lavish feast for everyone. Once the lady is married, her property becomes her husband's for as long as he lives. He has full rights over her. By law, he can beat her if he wishes (although not too harshly).

Peasant Weddings

The young lady and her noble friends in neighboring manors marry young. Peasant girls get married much later, usually in their twenties. They work as soon as they are able, and they do not marry until their grooms have some financial stability. If a peasant couple have children before they are married, the children kneel under the pall with their parents at the Nuptial (wedding) Mass. The priest declares the children legitimate—legal. After a peasant wedding, there is often a "bride-alc." The guests bring their own food to the celebration. The peasant women have to pay a sum of money to their local knight, the

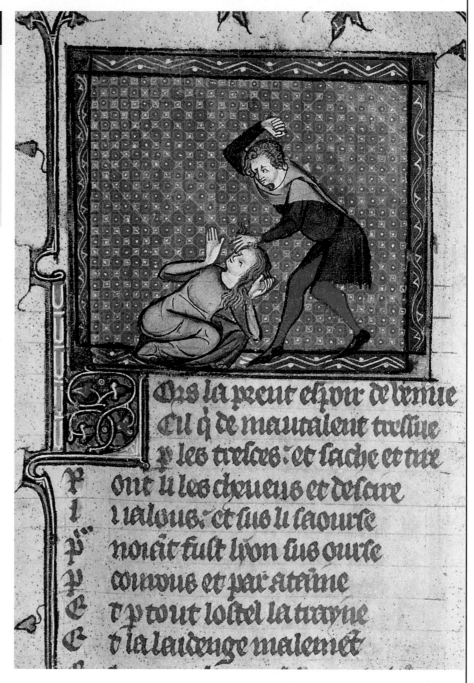

Married women had few rights in medieval times, and a husband could beat his wife.

lord of the manor, to allow them to get married. They could be fined by the knight for having children out of wedlock.

AT HOME

After the wedding, the lady lives in her new home. The manor house is built with thick walls of stone surrounded by a water-filled moat. Her husband is wealthy. Their shared home is large, although not as big as a castle. Only the most important nobles have castles.

Outside and Inside

The biggest room in the manor house is the Great Hall. Everyone eats their meals here, and the knight and his lady meet guests. The servants who work around the manor house sleep in the Great Hall at night on straw bedding. The knight and his lady are the only people with a private room, or "solar." Their bed is made up with fine linen. They have bowls of water to wash in—but no lavatory. Instead, there is a hole in the wall which is a garderobe. It has a chute beneath it to direct the refuse out into the moat. Outside there is a large courtyard and outbuildings such as stables, a henhouse, and a granary. The manor house and its buildings are fortified by a high wall and a moat to withstand possible attacks from enemies.

Meals were eaten in the Great Hall of a manor house and this is where the servants slept.

At her needlework

Overseeing the servants

At mass with the lord

With the gardener

Supervising the buying and storage of food

Self-Sufficiency

The following description characterizes some of the outbuildings of a manor granted to Robert Le Moyne in 1265. It shows how self-sufficient a manor house was. It had its own livestock and barns, as well as a henhouse, dairy, and granary.

❖ *Also two barns, one for wheat and one for oats. These buildings are enclosed with a moat, a wall, and a hedge. Also beyond the middle gate is a good barn and a stable for cows, and another for oxen, these old and ruinous. Also beyond the outer gate is a pigsty.* ❖

Manor Servants

The young lady of the manor gets to know all her servants and makes sure they do their work. As well as kitchen staff and gardeners, there are household staff who perform duties such as cleaning and lighting the fires in the rooms. It is important to keep the manor house clean to avoid grime and unpleasant smells. Both the lady and her husband have personal servants who help them dress and look after their clothing and personal well-being.

The servants receive a low pay, but they also get food and lodging. Most of the servants come from local peasant families on the estate, so they are known and trusted. On the occasional holidays, they can visit their families nearby.

Working in the Manor

It takes many servants to keep the manor running smoothly. The kitchen has large fireplaces to roast meat. A young servant has the job of turning the meat on a spit over the fires until it is cooked. There also are baking ovens. Outside there are vegetable gardens and livestock to look after.

The manor also has its own chapel where everyone goes to services led by the knight's personal priest, the chaplain. The knight's family sits in their own balcony above the servants.

BEING A WIFE

Advice Book

Christine de Pisan, a French noblewoman living in the fourteenth century, wrote *The Book of Three Virtues*. She advises women:

❖ *Because Barons and still more commonly knights and squires and gentlemen travel and go off to wars, their wives should be wise and sound administrators and manage their affairs well, because most of the time they stay at home without their husbands, who are at court or abroad.* ❖

The lady of the manor's husband is a knight. He is regularly called away for weeks at a time to fight for his lord. She must take charge of the house and the estate while he is away. She has been taught from childhood how to manage an estate, and one day she will teach her own daughter the same responsibilities.

Lady in Charge

The knight employs a steward, or manager, who helps to ensure the manor runs smoothly on a daily basis. He keeps an account of what is spent and makes sure there is enough food to feed everyone in the house. He also ensures the lands on the estate are well run. He reports problems to the knight. If the knight is away, he reports to the lady.

The lady is ultimately responsible for ensuring her servants and family are properly fed. She knows it is important to store a good harvest for the winter months when there will be much less for everyone to eat. She and the steward make sure enough farm animals are killed to provide meat that is preserved by smoking or salting. During the early 1300s, life is especially difficult. Freezing weather and food shortages are common throughout Europe. Everyone on the estate struggles to keep themselves fed during famines.

A lady had to plan carefully to ensure plentiful food was available at a feast.

Out on the Estate

The people who live on the knight's land must give him regular rent in money, goods, or work service. He employs a tax collector, a reeve, to collect what is owed. The reeve reports to the lady when the knight is away. If someone repeatedly fails to pay the reeve what they owe, they could be turned out of their home. The lady relies on the reeve and the steward to see problems coming and advise her what to do. The estate runs similar to a business with money coming in and going out. When her husband is away, the lady must be prepared to be the medieval version of a businesswoman.

Forced to Fight

A knight's wife is expected to defend her estate if it is attacked while her husband is away. Danger is more likely to come from a hostile neighboring knight than from a foreign invader. If a lady is called upon to do this, she must be prepared to quickly find weapons and organize the local people. Her husband, the knight, has trained local men to fight. They can mount a defense from inside the manor house walls using bows and arrows, clubs, and axes. Occasionally, medieval noblewomen might be called upon to defend their homes from a siege lasting weeks. They must organize not only the defense but ration the available food supply so that it lasts until the enemy gives up. This is more likely to happen if the noblewoman lives in an important castle.

The lady supervised many estate workers when her husband was absent.

Like her fellow noblewomen, the lady of the manor married young. She hopes to have as many children as possible so that at least one will survive to inherit her husband's estate. She knows, and fears, that some of her children will die at birth or from illnesses untreatable in medieval times.

Praying and Hoping

The lady prays to God to give her a child. When she is about to give birth, she prays to Saint Margaret, patron saint of childbirth. The lady wears a "birth girdle," a roll of parchment marked with prayers and a cross, which she thinks will help her with a safe delivery. Some religious houses and churches have relics or even the Virgin Mary's birth girdle. They lend these out to royalty and important aristocratic women when they are pregnant to "help" with the birth. Just like modern women, pregnant medieval women are given medical warnings. They are warned not to drink beer, eat pork, or ride on horseback to avoid harming the unborn baby.

Advice

A medieval poem, *How the Good Wife Taught her Daughter*, advises:
❖ *And when thou goest on thy way, go thou not too fast,*
Brandish not with thy head, nor with thy shoulders cast,
Have not too many words, from swearing keep aloof
For all such manners come to an evil proof. ❖

A medieval child clings to her noble mother in this manuscript painting.

This medieval oak cradle could be rocked gently back and forth.

Medieval Facts

There was no such thing as "baby food" in medieval times. Instead, women chewed the food before giving it to their toothless babies to eat.

The lady plays "knights" with her son as her husband's page (attendant) stands by.

A Dangerous Time

The lady has a local midwife to help her. This is a woman with some special knowledge of childbirth. Some medieval midwives are more skilled than others, and childbirth is a common cause of death among women of the time. Mothers-to-be are advised to confess their sins to a churchman before they go into labor, so that if they die, they will go to heaven.

New mothers stay at home. They only go out in public about a month after childbirth for a special church service called a churching, which is a purification ceremony. The new mother lights candles on the altar of Our Lady (Mary) as thanks for surviving. A churching ceremony has a party atmosphere, and all the women wear their best clothes. If rich noblewomen have churchings, they might have fine music and a big feast afterward.

Looking after the Children

The lady teaches her children and plays games with them, too. Her attendants share the childcare. Just as her brothers did, her sons leave when they are seven to become pages in another knight's household. From then on, she will only see them when they are given occasional holidays. She is in charge of two pages from someone else's family and teaches them manners and courtly ways. She also teaches her daughters how to be ladies. They must learn music, poetry, and embroidery—all the civilized skills expected of a noblewoman.

A YEAR IN THE LIFE

The lady's daily life, and the lives of all the people on her estate, varies according to the seasons. The land and the animals that everyone depends on to survive require year-round tending.

Yearly Celebrations

Every year, there are many holy days and festival days that are celebrated in different ways. Pentecost (Whit Sunday) is marked with a feast and a holiday. May Day (May 1) and Midsummer's Day (June 24) are among the days when there is a feast and people celebrate and relax. At Easter, the knight and his lady receive eggs from their tenants and give the servants a special dinner. Fairs may be held in the nearby town on festival days. Various stalls sell goods, and there is entertainment, such as wrestling competitions and music. The lady sends her servants to the fairs to buy unusual items that have been brought from abroad, such as spices and silks.

Christmastide

The two weeks from Christmas Eve to Twelfth Day (January 6) is Christmastide, the most important medieval holiday. The knight gives his manor staff bonuses at this time

Dancers dressed in green perform in the Great Hall at Christmastide as depicted in a fifteenth-century painting.

of year, such as extra clothing and firewood. The manor house is decorated with holly and ivy. Huge yule logs are brought in to keep the fire burning through the 12 days and nights of the celebration.

On Christmas morning, the lady's family goes to a service in the chapel. Then there is a feast, perhaps with a fine roasted boar to eat. At the end of the meal, the family tells riddles and sings Christmas songs. December 26 is Saint Stephen's Day. The family and their attendants play games outside in the yard, such as cockfighting and seeing who can leap the highest. Gifts are given at New Year. The lady might give her daughter an ivory comb or a ring. Her husband and sons might receive fine leather belts or linen handkerchiefs that were bought at the local fair and carefully stored away until Christmas.

A Lady's Day

On an ordinary day, the lady of the manor gets up soon after dawn. She puts on a piece of long underclothing called a chemise and washes her face in a bowl of water put out by her attendants. She dresses, with help from her servants, and goes to the chapel with the rest of her family to say mass. After breakfast, she must attend to estate matters, if her husband is away. The main meal of the day is at about 10:00 or 11:00 A.M. Then she likes to go hawking, riding, and hunting with birds of prey. After supper, she spends time in the solar reading, sewing, or talking by candlelight. Later, her attendants help her to prepare for bed. A fire is lit to keep the room warm. She washes with soap made from soda, wood ash, and animal fat. Although when she can get it, she buys luxury soap made abroad from olive oil and herbs. She says her prayers and goes to bed alongside her husband.

Two of the lady's favorite outdoor activities are riding and hawking with her husband.

Christmas Lunch

Christmas Day is celebrated in the medieval poem *Sir Gawain and the Green Knight*. This version is translated from the original Middle English:

❖ *There was meat and merrymaking and much delight.* ❖

CLOTHES AND HAIRSTYLES

There are rules about who wears what type of clothing. As a noblewoman, the lady can wear fine clothes studded with jewels, like clothing worn by the royal court. People from lower classes are strictly discouraged from wearing anything that makes them appear to be above their rank. The lower a person is on the social ladder, the simpler is the clothing.

Fashion trend – a lady of the French court.

A Lady's Clothing

The lady wears several layers of clothing. Over her chemise she wears two long tunics, one with short sleeves over one with longer sleeves. She might wear a mantle—a short cape. Her clothes are made of wool or linen. The material is sometimes sent home by her husband when he is fighting abroad. There are no ready-made clothes to purchase. She must buy lengths of material and pay a seamstress to make her clothes. She wears a girdle (a belt that hangs down at the front), a necklace and rings, and flat shoes with pointed toes.

Hair and Headdresses

When she was unmarried, the lady of the manor wore her hair without a veil. Now she covers her head with a veil called a wimple that flows down the back of her head. It is secured around her face with pins and worn with a circlet on top. Her hair is worn long underneath. Her servants sometimes redden her lips with ochre—made from powdered clay—and whiten her skin a bit by dusting it with flour.

She eagerly listens to news about fashions at court, which often change to echo new trends seen abroad. Clothing in her time is mostly red, green, or blue. Later in the fourteenth century, plum and tan will become fashionable colors. By the end of the century, black becomes the preferred color for every noble.

Medieval Fashion

Fashion changes often in medieval times, and it is usually based on the styles worn by royalty. When the lady was young, in the early 1300s, clothing was simple. Now, in the 1320s, long downward-pointing sleeves and lots of little buttons are the height of fashion. Later on, medieval women will wear clothes that are much more embroidered, wide wirework headdresses that are covered in fabric, and even tall steeple-shaped hats.

Noblemen are just as interested in fashion. One year they wear long robes, the next shorter ones. Hairstyles change too—long hair, then collar-length hair, small hoods and then long pointed ones. Men wear short beards, sometimes forked. They wear pointed shoes, finely decorated leather belts, and jewelry.

Fashionably dressed nobles, depicted in a Burgundian prayer book of the early fifteenth century.

23

The lady of the manor has time to embroider, read, and go hawking with her own trained bird of prey. She enjoys games such as chess, which she plays with her attendants. She likes to keep a few pets—a small dog and some birds in a cage.

Servants in attendance (one holding a hawk) as the lord and lady prepare to go out.

Accomplishments

A thirteenth-century poem by Robert De Blois describes his ideal medieval heroine:

❖ *She could carry and fly a falcon, tersel and hawk,*
She knew well how to play chess and tables (backgammon),
How to read romances, tell tales and sing songs. ❖

Hawking for Women

When the lady goes out riding with her husband and servants, her bird of prey is perched on her gloved hand. She lets it loose to catch small prey, such as rabbits. Her bird has been trained by the falconer, but she has spent a lot of time with it so it is used to her. Hawking has many social rules. Different types of people are expected to have particular species of hunting birds. Owning a bird above your rank is considered rebellious. Ladies are allowed a merlin, a breed of falcon.

Music and Games

The lady plays music or sings, and she enjoys chess. In the medieval rules, the pieces move differently than in modern rules. The game of backgammon is also popular. On special occasions, there are party games. In hot cockles, players took turns striking a player who is blindfolded. The blindfolded player had to identify each person who struck them. The lady has heard that the wealthiest people play card games, but she does not possess any. The cards come from the Middle East; they are hand painted and very expensive.

24

A noble couple play backgammon in this fourteenth-century manuscript painting.

Sewing and Spinning

To while away winter evenings, the lady embroiders on a frame. She uses silks that she sent her servants to buy from a peddler who travels from village to village, carrying his wares on a cart. She knows how to make woolen thread. She spins it by hand using a spindle—a stick with a weight attached to it. The richer the nobles, the more fine woven wool tapestries they can afford to hang on their walls. These are made by specialty weavers in town and city workshops. A fine tapestry hangs in the solar depicting hunting scenes. It helps to keep the cold out of the stone-walled room, and the lady enjoys its bright colors. It is a treasure that will be passed down through the family.

BOOKS

Like many medieval ladies, the lady has her own collection of books. These help fill the time she spends in the solar. She loves books of poetry and romance. She also has a religious primer—a book of prayers for every occasion. Her favorite book is a collection of French tales of brave knights and beautiful ladies. All her books have been copied by hand and are very precious.

Chivalry and Women

In books and poetry of the time, chivalry is a strong theme. The chivalrous heroes of knightly adventures worship women as pure and holy creatures to be protected and admired. This tradition is called "courtly love." Women sometimes are portrayed as untrustworthy magical creatures or evil witches disguising themselves as pretty ladies to trick knights into sin and ruin. A knight must be on guard for these types of women and keep himself pure.

The lady and her attendants love to listen to traveling minstrels. These troubadours occasionally arrive in her area and sing songs of courtly love and magical adventures.

Medieval Facts

Medieval noblewomen often left their precious books to their loved ones in their wills, so we know what was in their collections. For instance, the Countess of Devon's will, made in 1390, left her daughters her primer, a book of medicines, and some tales of Merlin and King Arthur.

A noble lady reading. In the medieval period, bookshelves had not yet been invented. Books were kept safely in chests and then put on a stand for reading.

Women Writers

The lady reads her books out loud to her children and to her women friends. They are written in Norman French or in Middle English, the name for the English language used at the time. A few medieval stories and poems are written by women, such as the poet Marie de France, writing in the twelfth century. In the fourteenth century, the world's first professional woman writer, Christine de Pisan, is at work in France. As a young widow with three children to look after, she makes a living from writing successful lifestyle advice books for women.

What Women Learn

Noblewomen are taught how to behave from books of manners and advice. Possessing good manners, being religious, and knowing how to run a good household is the basis of a noblewoman's education.

Her books reflect that. But many believe that too much learning is harmful to women. The medieval Spanish king, Phillippe of Navarre, forbids women to read or write, in case they read corrupting romance stories or start writing love letters.

The Wife of Bath

Geoffrey Chaucer wrote *The Canterbury Tales* in the fourteenth century. The Wife of Bath complains that most medieval stories are written by men who invariably make the women appear to be the wicked ones. This version is translated into modern English:

❖ *By God, if women had but written stories,*
Like those the clergy keep in their rooms.
More would have been written of man's wickedness
Than all the sons of Adam could redress. ❖

The French author Christine de Pisan writing in her study is depicted in a fourteenth-century manuscript painting.

TIME TO EAT

The lady eats better than many of the people who live on the manor because she is of noble birth. The meat, milk, and crops of her husband's estate are available. But in famine times, when crops fail and animals die, everyone in the manor will go hungry, including the nobles.

Food at the Manor

The knight and his family have three meals a day. In a good farming year, there will be plenty to eat. There are vegetables and herbs from the garden; beef, pork and lamb; birds such as chickens and wildfowl; and fish from the local streams. Milled flour is used to make white bread. Cheese and butter are made in the dairy. Everyone drinks ale or milk as the water supply is not clean.

Animals such as wild boar, deer, and rabbits live on the estate woodlands and are hunted for food. They are the knight's property and peasants are forbidden from hunting them. If caught, they will be severely punished, perhaps by being put in the stocks.

A well-off family eats a meal in the Great Hall of their home. A linen cloth covers the table; the plates and vessels are of pewter. A servant brings in the different courses.

The Cook

Geoffrey Chaucer describes a cook in *The Canterbury Tales* written in the fourteenth century. This version is translated into modern English:
❖ *They had a Cook with them who stood alone,*
For boiling chicken with a marrow-bone,
Sharp flavoring-powder and a spice for savor.
He could distinguish London ale by flavor,
And he could roast and seethe and broil and fry,
Make good thick soup and bake a tasty pie.
But what a pity — so it seemed to me,
That he should have an ulcer on his knee. ❖

Medieval Facts

The medieval diet was not healthy. It was low in some important vitamins, and fruit was considered to be bad for one's health. This is opposite of what we now know to be true. On the other hand, the medieval diet was generally low in fat, unlike the diets of many people today.

A noble hunting party sets off. Game was an important source of food in medieval times.

For instance, once a bird is cooked, its feathers may be replaced and the bird posed so it looks alive. Birds such as larks, thrushes, finches, peacocks, sea gulls, and cormorants can be roasted. Delicious puddings and spiced wines are also offered.

Sweet and savory tastes are often mixed together. An example is a popular dish called "blankmanger." This milky stew is made from chicken paste, flour, almonds, milk, and sugar or honey. At a feast, exotic expensive foods from abroad, such as figs, dates, and oranges, might be served.

Peasant Food

Most peasants on the manor do not have access to milled wheat flour. Wheat only grows on the best land, so they make a heavy dark bread from barley and rye. After a poor harvest, they might need to add acorns or beans to their bread recipe. The main meal is pottage, a thick soup made of vegetables and herbs. Oats, and sometimes bacon, are added. Everything must be preserved as well as possible for the winter months by salting, smoking, or soaking in salt water. Pigs are free to run around and eat whatever they can find. They make an ideal cheap animal for peasants to keep through the summer and kill for winter.

A Feast Day

A medieval feast is a grand occasion. Many food courses and luxuries show the guests how wealthy the host is. When the knight hosts a feast, he and his wife sit at the high table in the Great Hall, along with their important guests. All kinds of meat and fish courses are served, along with "subtleties." These are foods disguised as something else.

When anyone in the lady's family falls ill, she sends word to the local monastery for help and advice. The monks provide medical care as much as they are able. The lady relies on their knowledge of healing herbs to produce homemade medicines they hope will help.

To Make a Salve

Most medicines used plants. This medieval recipe describes how to make a salve to be put on the skin:

❖ *Take two handfuls of mallows, one handful each of milfoil, fennel, and dwarf elder, three handfuls of leaves of leeks. Let them be cut very minutely, ground and roasted with a little water.* ❖

"Herbals" indicated which plants were medicinally useful. Shown is marigold.

All About Humors

Like everyone in her time, the lady believes that the world is made up of four elements called the "humors." These are fire, air, earth, and water and correspond in the body as blood, yellow bile, black bile, and phlegm. Illness is thought to occur when there is too much of a humor in the body.

Women, thought to be deficient in heat, are said to be weaker in mind and body. Their lack of heat is said to account for their untrustworthy nature, and they are thought to suffer from more illnesses than men. Like other women of her time, the lady must put up with some negative attitudes toward women in both medicine and religion.

Religion or Ritual?

In the local monastery, there is a small hospital wing for very sick men. Women are cared for in the nunnery. The abbess of the local convent has a good knowledge of medicine, and there are women healers in one or two of the local villages. Like the monks and nuns, they use herbs and ground-up stones to create homemade cures. They often add some ancient rituals, such as picking herbs when facing south at sunrise to make them stronger or chanting an old charm as they pick herbs.

Such old healing rituals are unpopular with the church because they are similar to ancient pre-Christian beliefs, but local people still privately rely on them. The church teaches that illness is partly due to sin, so sick people often visit religious shrines to pray for forgiveness and thus a cure.

Bloodletting and Cupping

A common treatment for illness is bloodletting. This rids the body of too much heat that is thought to

occur if someone is feverish or has an infection. Barbers also perform basic surgery and dentistry. The barber can cut open the patient in a way that leads to some blood loss that is not too harmful.

Another common treatment is cupping. Glass cups are put on the skin to draw blood to the surface to reduce the pressure of having "too much blood."

The lady uses a few herbal remedies from her garden to cure her family of minor problems. She treats them with lemon balm for colds, marjoram for bruises, lungwort for a cough, and feverfew for headaches. Since she is quite wealthy, she is able to buy tooth powder made from crushed seashells and rubs it on her teeth to clean them. Others in her household do not clean their teeth and have rotting teeth as a result.

A lady stirs medicine over the fire for her husband, who is recovering from illness.

In the local towns and villages, there are peasant women who live very differently than the lady of the manor. If she meets them, they treat her with great deference knowing she is much grander than they are. They live a life of hard work and sometimes poverty and starvation during famine times. They generally die much younger than noblewomen.

This picture of a peasant woman selling leeks is from a 1356 Italian manuscript.

A Peasant Wife

A peasant is someone who lives by farming a small piece of land and paying the local knight rent, tax, or work services for it. If peasants get behind on their payments, they will lose the land and be thrown out. A typical medieval peasant family consists of a wife, husband, and two or three children. They live in a small house along with their animals. A peasant's wife is his partner in work as well as in marriage. She helps to farm the land as well as look after the family. Young peasant girls usually marry later than noblewomen because their families need them to work for a while to help earn money.

Artisan Women

The next step up in society from a peasant is an artisan, someone who makes a living by a trade or craft. It is possible for a single or widowed woman to become a successful artisan in her own right. If she earns enough money, she can buy land, run a market stall, or perhaps run a shop in a local town. Eventually, she might be wealthy enough to have servants of her own. Women often work as brewers, since everyone drinks ale instead of the unclean water. Some women make a living from practical skills such as weaving or bookbinding. There are a few women craftworkers, such as artists. Trades such as butchers, goldsmiths, and shoemakers may have female members. Most of these women work alongside their fathers or husbands.

The French artist Thamar (Timarete) painting a picture in about 1400.

Christine de Pisan, a fourteenth-century Frenchwoman, wrote this advice for the wives of artisans in *The Book of Three Virtues:*
❖ *Urging the others to action, she herself should put her hand to the task, making sure that she knows the craft so well she can direct the workmen if her husband is not there.* ❖

Working for the Nobles

From about the age of 12, some peasant girls might be selected to work in the local manor house. They might be laundresses, dairymaids, or helpers in the kitchen. They begin with the lowliest tasks and gradually go up in rank, until they marry and leave the manor to run their own home. Their pay is low, but food and shelter is provided. Outside the manor house, their life would be more difficult, especially in times of famine and disease.

Once a woman married, all her property went to her husband. But in some parts of England, such as London, Exeter, or Lincoln, married women had extra rights and could run their own businesses without their husband owning everything.

The lady of the manor occasionally visits the castle of her husband's lord, the nobleman who grants him his land and title. She meets the lord's wife who is related to royalty and is from a higher-born family than her own. Important aristocratic women are the female celebrities of their day, setting fashion trends for clothing and behavior that other women follow.

Queen Isabel of France enters Paris; a painting from a fourteenth-century manuscript.

The Baroness

Christine de Pisan, writing in the fourteenth century, gave advice to highborn women in *The Book of Three Virtues.*

❖ *These women must be highly knowledgeable about government and wise. . . . The knowledge of a baroness must be so comprehensive that she can understand everything. . . . Moreover she must have the courage of a man.* ❖

Castle Life

The life of a highborn aristocratic woman is different than that of a lesser-ranked lady of the manor. Her home is much larger, and there are many more servants. Her daily life involves less duties around the estate and more leisure time for reading poetry, hunting, and enjoying music. She might entertain guests at lavish feasts and tournaments. Perhaps, she may even play host to the king and the court. Her clothes are made of the finest materials; her hair is arranged in the latest fashion of the court. She is expected to be a patron—a financial backer and supporter—of poetry and art. She is also expected to give generously to charity. Highborn aristocratic women sometimes donate large sums of money to found new nunneries.

Fourteenth-century ladies watch a jousting match. Jousting was dangerous and many nobles were killed or injured.

Tournament Times

Grand ladies play an important part in the ritual of tournaments—competitions between jousting knights. A lord might hold a tournament and invite knights to take part. The lady of the manor looks forward to these rare, but splendid, events and hopes that her husband will not get hurt. The noble female spectators have their own stand. They give favors, such as circlets of flowers or handkerchiefs, to their favorite contestants to wear during the jousting bouts. The lady of the castle gives out the prizes, and the winner is declared her champion. Dances are held and the knights vie with each other to charm the women with their courtly manners.

Powerful and Dangerous

Highborn aristocratic women can be politically powerful, doing their best to maneuver their family into more power. Sometimes they interfere too much and get into trouble.

The lady and her friends have been talking about the scandalous behavior of Isabella, wife of King Edward II. Neglected by her husband, she recently took her son to France where she rallied support and invaded England. She deposed her husband. It is said she had him murdered at Berkeley Castle in Gloucestershire in 1327, so that she and her lover, Roger Mortimer, could rule on behalf of her young son.

THE LADY AND THE NUNS

If she had not married, the lady of the manor might have considered becoming a nun, one of the few careers open to noblewomen. As it is, like all noblewomen, she is expected to give money and gifts to her local nunnery. In return, the nuns pray for her soul.

Women at the Nunnery

Medieval nunneries are much smaller than monasteries, and there are fewer of them around the country. A nunnery might be home to 20 or 30 nuns, or even as few as 10. Their leader is an abbess or prioress and only the daughters of nobles or merchants become nuns.

The nunnery might offer some teaching for local noble girls in return for money. It also provides a boarding house for noblewomen who wish to stay for a while, although the church disapproves of this. Rich noblewomen sometimes retire to a nunnery in later life and are looked after by the nuns.

A nun uses her rosary—the string of beads—to help her pray.

36

A Nun's Life

A nun takes a vow of chastity and spends the rest of her life living in the nunnery. She wears nun's clothing covering her head and body. Every day is a strict routine of prayer, study, work, and perhaps tending the nunnery gardens or farm. There are seven religious services daily; the first is at 2:00 A.M. Then the nuns can go back to bed until 6:00 A.M. when the day properly starts. There are six more services to attend until 7:00 or 8:00 P.M., when the nuns go to bed.

Naughty Nuns

Nuns are often criticized by churchmen. Common complaints include nuns not saying prayers properly, taking too much interest in fashionable clothes, wearing expensive jewelry, dancing, playing party games, and keeping pets and taking them into church. One story tells of a bishop who visits a nunnery and demands that the pet dogs be removed. But once the bishop has gone away, the nuns whistle and the dogs return. Nuns are not really meant to go outside the convent, but they often do. Sometimes, they visit monasteries.

Medieval nuns sing a religious service in the choir stalls of their convent.

THE WORLD OUTSIDE

The lady of the manor has never traveled much outside her local area. She has certainly never been outside of England.

What she knows of the world comes from her books and what she has been told by her husband about his time spent abroad.

This thirteenth-century map depicts Europe, Africa, and Asia. North is on the left, the Mediterranean Sea is at the middle bottom.

Dangers on the Road

Traveling is quite difficult. The roads are often badly rutted and can make a horse lame. If the roads are flooded or icy, the way may be impassable. There are no signposts. Often, the roads are no more than muddy tracks. There are wolves and wild boars. There are also gangs of outlaws—men who have escaped from the law and now lurk in the countryside looking for travelers to rob. The lady of the manor would never think of traveling alone. When she decides to go on a pilgrimage, she takes armed servants with her for security.

A Holy Pilgrimage

The lady has heard older noblewomen, especially widows, speak of their pilgrimages. She decides to make her own pilgrimage to a local shrine. It is dedicated to Mary, mother of Jesus, who is said to have appeared in visions and caused miracle medical cures. On the journey, the lady and her servants stay in nunneries and inns. When she arrives at the holy site, she gives

money to help the poor and buys candles for the shrine. Like other medieval pilgrims, she is sure her journey will wipe away her sins and help her to get into heaven.

More adventurous travelers go all the way to Santiago de Compostela, Spain, the most popular medieval pilgrimage site in Europe where the bones of the disciple Saint James are said to rest.

When she travels, the lady rides in a litter slung between two horses.

Medieval Facts

Foreign goods, such as spices and silks, reach Europe by North African traveling traders. These are expensive luxuries that only the nobility can afford.

A Small World

Medieval people have little knowledge of the world outside Europe. The lady knows of France, Spain, and other parts of Europe. She is aware of the Holy Lands and the crusades that took place in earlier medieval times. She knows vaguely of Asia because of trade links between China and Europe. She knows nothing of the rest of

Africa, America, or Australia. She assumes the known world is entirely surrounded by oceans.

The lady is afraid of anyone who is not a Christian. She has been taught by the church that all non-Christian people are enemies of the Christian Catholic kingdoms of Europe.

WIDOWHOOD

The lady of the manor's husband dies when she is 35. She is now a widow. Widowhood is common in medieval times because of the high mortality rate. Although saddened by her husband's death, she now has more wealth and legal rights than at any other time in her life.

Free and Rich

When her husband dies, all of the lady's property returns to her, including the dower land she brought with her on her marriage. She also gets a third of her husband's personal goods. A third goes to his children and a third to the church for the good of his soul. Her eldest son inherits the estate. Widows are supposed to be respected ladies of the community, but they also have a reputation for a love of fine living.

Problems of Widowhood

In earlier times, a rich noble's widow could be given in marriage to whomever the king chose, unless she paid a fine to marry

This medieval wax seal belonged to a noble lady. It is a strong image of a powerful and independent woman.

whom she wished. This was a lucrative tax that brought the king a lot of money. But the law has changed, and widows now can manage their own estate. They can spend their money as they like without being forced to give it to an unwanted new husband. Some widowed noblewomen choose to live in a nunnery and pay to be looked after.

A Medieval Death

After a short illness, the lady dies in 1343 at 52—a good age for a woman in medieval times. In her will, she leaves her books to her daughter, who also inherits her dower land. She leaves some of her possessions to her favorite tenants and servants. She had chosen to be buried next to her husband in the local church. She has had an effigy—a brightly painted carving—made of her to be placed beside the effigy of her husband. His effigy shows him in full armor. Her carving shows her in a fashionable gown. After a grand funeral, the lady is laid to rest next to her husband.

The Black Death

Sweeping across Europe in 1348-49, the disease known as the Black Death—thought to be plague— killed as much as one-third of the population. By dying in 1343, our lady of the manor escaped the horrors of the dreadful disease that spared neither men, women, nor children.

❧

A noble lady's grave is marked by a stone effigy in the local parish church. The paint has worn off this effigy.

GLOSSARY

Abbess ❖ the head of a religious community of nuns

Artisan ❖ a craftsperson, who makes a living from a skill such as weaving or candle making

Banns ❖ a wedding announcement that must be read on three separate occasions in a church before a wedding can take place

Baptize ❖ to pronounce a baby a member of the Christian Church—it was believed unbaptized people could not go to heaven

Betrothal ❖ a marriage arrangement when young people are promised to each other; in medieval times, a noble woman had no choice in whom she married

Black Death ❖ the name given to the plague that ravaged Europe in the late 1340s

Bloodletting ❖ cutting open someone to allow blood to flow out

Catholic ❖ the religion of all Europe in medieval times, headed by the pope

Chaplain ❖ a personal priest who provides religious instruction and services for a noble family

Chemise ❖ a lady's loose undergarment similar to a dress

Chivalry ❖ a code of honorable behavior that knights were meant to follow

Churching ❖ a special church service held to purify a medieval woman after she has given birth

Coat-of-arms ❖ the official badge of a noble family

Courtly love ❖ the pure and chivalrous admiration of women, as set out in medieval poems and stories of brave knights

Cupping ❖ cups put on the skin to draw blood to the surface

Disciple ❖ one of the 12 closest followers of Jesus Christ

Dower land ❖ land given to a bride by her family when she marries

Dowry ❖ money and goods given to the groom by a bride's family when she marries

Estate ❖ land and properties owned by a nobleman

Famine ❖ mass starvation caused when crops fail

Garderobe ❖ a medieval toilet—a hole in the wall with a chute leading outside

Girdle ❖ a belt worn by a medieval woman; its ends hang down at the front

Great Hall ❖ the large main room in a castle or manor where meetings were held and meals were eaten

Hawking ❖ hunting with birds of prey (now called falconry)

Heir ❖ someone who is first in line to receive land, goods, and perhaps a noble title passed down to them on their parents' death

Humors ❖ elements thought to be in the body, corresponding to fire, earth, air, and water

Inheritance ❖ land, money, and sometimes a noble title handed on by a relative when they die; in medieval times, the oldest son was always first in line to inherit everything

Joust ❖ a tournament where two knights rode toward each other and scored points by striking their opponent with a lance

Knight ❖ a lesser-ranked noble who owes allegiance (loyalty) to a lord

Limbo ❖ a miserable place between heaven and hell where unbaptized babies were said to go

Lord ❖ a highly ranked nobleman

Manor house ❖ a nobleman's home, smaller than a castle

Mantle ❖ a short cloak

Medieval ❖ the period of history approximately between 1000 and 1500

Merlin ❖ a type of small hawk used by medieval ladies for hunting

Middle English ❖ a medieval form of the English language

Monastery ❖ a religious community of monks

Norman ❖ something or someone connected to the French forces that invaded England in 1066, led by William the Conqueror from Normandy; a castle described as Norman means it was built by the invaders

Nunnery ❖ a religious community of nuns

Our Lady ❖ the Virgin Mary, mother of Jesus

Pagan ❖ pre-Christian religion and rituals

Page ❖ a young boy aged seven or more who served a knight and his family while learning to be a knight

Patron ❖ a financial backer

Peasant ❖ a poor person with no rank who makes a living farming land belonging to a noble

Pilgrimage ❖ a trip to a holy shrine

Pottage ❖ a thick soup made from vegetables

Primer ❖ a book of prayers

Reeve ❖ a knight's tax collector

Shrine ❖ a holy site, visited by pilgrims

Steward ❖ a knight's household assistant who helped him manage his estate

Solar ❖ a private family room above the Great Hall

Tapestry ❖ a decorative woven wall hanging

Tenant ❖ someone who rents land or property belonging to someone else

Wimple ❖ a veil worn off the face, draped down the back of the head

Work service ❖ days of labor given to a lord as a form of rent

Yule log ❖ a giant log that burns throughout Christmastide

Useful Medieval History Web Sites

www.fordham.edu/halsall/sbook.html

A Web site where you can read many original documents.

http://www.oxfordshirepast.net/ml_man.html

This Web site describes two English manors and includes photographs of the buildings.

http://www.medieval-life.net/life_main.htm

This Web site describes life during medieval times. It includes topics such as clothing, food, health, tournaments, and education.

www.mnsu.edu/emuseum/history/middleages/

A Web site where you can focus on life as a medieval peasant, knight, nun, or merchant.

Note to parents and teachers:

Every effort has been made by the publishers to ensure that the Web sites in this book are suitable for children, that they are of the highest educational value, and that they contain no inappropriate or offensive material. However, because of the nature of the Internet, it is impossible to guarantee that the contents of these sites will not be altered. We strongly advise that Internet access be supervised by a responsible adult.

TIME LINE

ca. 1000	Europe experiences a great expansion in its population over the next 200 years.
ca. 1000	A heavier wheeled plow, which cuts deeper, replaces the lighter hook plow and more horses are used in farming.
1066	William of Normandy invades England and is crowned king in December.
1096	The First Crusade begins.
ca. 1100	Over the next 200 years, there is a great expansion of peasant settlement.
ca. 1100	Gradual introduction of the three-field agricultural system across much of northern Europe.
1135–1154	Civil war breaks out in England.
1146–1254	The Second through Seventh Crusades occur.
1150	Knights begin to use coats-of-arms.
ca. 1190	The first windmills are built in Europe.
ca. 1200	Some peasant houses are built of stone in northern Europe.
ca. 1200	Horses replace cattle to pull heavy loads in northern Europe.
ca. 1200	Money rents replace labor services across Europe. There is a growth in towns, trade, and the economy.
1205	The River Thames freezes and can be crossed over the ice.
1207	The Order of St. Francis is formed in Italy.
1208	King John quarrels with the pope; church services are banned in England.
1215	King John signs the Magna Carta that gives the nobles more power.
1260	The cathedral is consecrated at Chartres in France.
1265	Marco Polo travels to the Far East.
1279	England introduces new silver coins.
1285	Spectacles are made in northern Italy.
ca. 1310	The mechanical clock is perfected.
1317	Europe experiences heavy rain and ruined harvests; famine spreads across Europe.
1323–1328	The peasants revolt in the Netherlands.
1337	The Hundred Years' War between England and France begins.
1344	The English make their first gold coin.
1346	The French are defeated at the Battle of Crécy.
1348–1349	The bubonic plague (Black Death) spreads through Europe.
1361	Europe experiences another outbreak of the plague.
1362	William Langland begins to write his poem Piers Plowman.
1369	Harvests fail across Europe.
1381	The Peasant's Revolt occurs in England.
1387	Chaucer begins *The Canterbury Tales*.
1388	The first town sanitation act is passed in the English parliament.
1430–1470	Economic crises hit England; many peasants are ruined.
1437–1438	Many parts of Europe experience the plague and famine.
1438–1440	England experiences heavy rain and ruined harvests.
1453	The Hundred Years' War ends.
1470	An economic revival begins.
1500	Knights no longer go to war—their main role is that of a landowner.

INDEX

A

aristocrat 18, 34, 35
artisans 32, 33
artists 32, 33

B

banns, wedding 12
baptism 10
betrothal 12
birds (of prey) 21, 24
Black Death 41, 43
bloodletting 31
books 26, 27, 38

C

Canterbury Tales, The 27, 28, 37, 43
castles 14, 17, 34, 35
Chaucer, Geoffrey 27, 28, 37, 43
childbirth 10, 18, 19
children 10, 18, 19
chivalry, code of 26
Christmastide 20, 21
church 10, 12, 18, 19, 31, 36, 37, 39, 40, 41
churching 19
clothing 11, 15, 19, 21, 22, 34, 37
coat-of-arms 11
court, royal 22, 34
craftworkers 32
crusades 8, 39, 43
cupping 31
custody 11

D

de Pisan, Christine 16, 27, 33, 34
diet, medieval 28, 29
dower 11, 12, 40, 41
dowry 12

E

education 19, 27
Edward I 9
Edward II 35
Eleanor of Aquitaine 35
embroidery 11, 19, 21, 24, 25

estate, the 9, 11, 12, 15, 16, 17, 18, 20, 21, 28, 34, 40, 41

F

famine 16, 28, 32, 33, 43
farming 28, 29, 32, 43
fashion 22, 23, 34
feasts 13, 16, 19, 20, 21, 29, 34
festivals 20
feudalism 8, 9

G/H/I

games 19, 21, 24, 25
garderobe 14
Great Hall 14, 20, 28, 29
hairstyles 22, 23, 34
hawking 21, 24
herbs 21, 28, 29, 30, 31
hobbies 24
holidays 15, 19, 20, 21
Holy Lands 39
humors 30
Hundred Years' War 8, 43
hunting 21, 25, 28, 29, 34
illness 18, 30, 31
inheritance 11, 12, 17, 18, 40, 41

J/K/L

jousts 35
kings 8, 9, 11, 34, 35, 40, 41, 43
knights 8, 17, 19, 26, 28, 29, 32, 35, 43
ladies, aristocratic 18, 34, 35
lady of the manor,
    birth 10, 11
    childhood 10, 11
    children 18, 19
    daily life 14, 21
    death 41
    education 11, 27
    funeral 41
    leisure 20, 21, 24, 25
    marriage 9, 12, 13, 40
    running the estate 15, 16, 17
    widowhood 40, 41

M

makeup 22, 23
manners 11, 19, 27, 35
manor house 10, 14, 15, 17, 21, 33
map 38
mass 21
medicine 26, 30, 31
midwives 10, 19
minstrels 26
monasteries 30, 31, 36, 37
music 11, 19, 20, 24, 26, 34

N/P

nunneries 31, 34, 36, 37, 39, 41
nuns 31, 36, 37
pages 11, 19
patrons 34, 35
peasants 8, 9, 13, 15, 28, 29, 32, 33, 43
pilgrimage 39
priests 13, 15
primer 26

R

reading 11, 21, 24, 26, 27, 34
reeve 16
remedies 30, 31
rights, women's 9, 13, 33, 40

S

servants 14, 15, 16, 20, 21, 22, 24, 25, 28, 34, 39, 41
shrine 31, 39
solar 10, 14, 21, 25, 26
stewards 16

T/W

tournaments, jousting 34, 35
travel 38, 39
wars 8, 16, 43
weaving 25, 32
wedding 12, 13
widows 11, 27, 32, 39, 40, 41
William the Conqueror 8, 43
women, working 32, 33

These are the lists of contents for each title in *Medieval Lives*:

Peasant
Introduction · First Years · Peasant Cottage · Childhood
The Church · Marriage · Land · Work Service for the Manor · The Manorial Court
The Working Year · Feeding the Family · Sickness and Health · Women's Work · Earning Money
Games and Entertainment · Freedom · Last Days · Glossary · Time Line/Useful Web Sites · Index

Merchant
Introduction · First Days · House and Home · Growing Up · School · Becoming a Merchant
Marriage · The Wool Trade · Travel and Communication · War and Piracy · Secrets of Success
Branching Out · Wealth and Property · Merchant's Wife · Good Works · Health and Diet
The End · Glossary · Time Line/Useful Web Sites · Index

Knight
All About Knights · A Future Knight Is Born · Time to Leave Home · Becoming a Squire
A Squire Goes Forth · Becoming a Knight · Invitation to the Castle · Joust! · Called to War
Battlefield Tactics · Dressed to Kill · Weapons · Siege Warfare · Pilgrimage · Returning Home
Knightly Duties · Death of a Knight · Glossary · Time Line/Useful Web Sites · Index

Nun
Introduction · Birth · Childhood and Education · To the Nunnery — Postulant
The Nunnery · Taking the Veil — Novice · Daily Life — the Offices · The Inner Life
Daily Routine · Enclosure · Cellaress and Librarian · The World Outside · Priests and Nuns
Poverty and Personal Possessions · A Visitation · Difficult Times · Death · Glossary
Time Line/Useful Web Sites · Index

Lady of the Manor
A Medieval Lady · Beginnings · Invitation to a Wedding
At Home · Being a Wife · Noble Children · A Year in the Life
Clothes and Hairstyles · Sports and Hobbies · Books · Time to Eat · Treating Illness
Women Who Work · The Noblest Ladies · The Lady and the Nuns · The World Outside
Widowhood · Glossary · Time Line/Useful Web Sites · Index

Stonemason
Introduction · Birth · Childhood and Growing Up · Training at the Quarry
Training at the Building Site · Working as a Rough Mason · Summoned to Work at a Castle
A Real Mason at the Abbey · A Growing Reputation · Stone Carver · The Lodge
Under Mason for the College · Master Mason for the Cathedral · Designing the Cathedral
Building the Cathedral · Fulfillment and Retirement · End of a Life ·
Glossary · Time Line/Useful Web Sites · Index